Children, Fire, and Intervention

Creating a Program that Saves Lives and Communities

Kathleen L. Stone

Dedication

I want to thank my husband, Gary, and our friend, Corey Dean, for launching our department's Youth Firesetter Intervention program. You were the first to see the need and sought out training to meet that need. I would never have become aware of how prevalent the problem of youth and fire is if it hadn't been for you. You inspired me to get involved!

ISBN–13: 978-1532999819
ISBN-10: 153299981X

Forward

Understanding that fire and burns are the leading cause of injury and death to children, gives reason that every fire department has the need for a youth fire setter's intervention program. *Children, Fire, and Intervention* is the kind of book that every fire department should have in their library. A must read for anyone who has the desire to help save lives and property in their community by addressing the growing need for youth fire setter intervention.

The author, Kathleen L. Stone, does the research for you and delivers an easy to understand, step-by-step guide to create an intervention program. Our fire department, West Thurston Regional Fire Authority, and Community are blessed to have such an experienced professional, champion our intervention program. Kathy has been a public school educator in western Washington since 1978. Her experience in the fire service, as a professional educator, and as a Firesetter Intervention Specialist (since 2006) gives her the knowledge and experience necessary to simplify the process for anyone who has the interest to start a Youth Firesetter Intervention program.

Kathy is one of only a few intervention specialists in our region and often serves the larger region as the expert intervention specialist. She has been called on countless times by other fire departments, as well the judicial and social service systems in the State of Washington. Kathy's motivation is clear; she knows that fire setter intervention resources are sparse, because many of us are uncertain of how to provide meaningful intervention. Many fire departments avoid their responsibility by passing it on to someone else. Before Kathy and her husband, Gary, developed our program our department also avoided the reasonability or at best a firefighter would scold the child, which at the time was our limited understanding of fire setter intervention. Well no more excuses! You could give this book to anyone … social worker, firefighter, parent or fire chief and by using the resources and following the lesson plan they could deliver a well-planned and effective intervention in no time. The comprehensive age appropriate lessons, interview techniques and resources in the book really make it as easy as following the step-by-step directions in a cookbook when making a meal for the first time.

Russell Kaleiwahea, Fire Chief
West Thurston Regional Fire Authority

Table of Contents

Youth Fire Setting ... A Growing Concern

Fire setting by children under the age of eighteen is a growing problem in communities across our nation. Almost every child has some curiosity about fire but lack understanding of its true nature. Three- to five-year olds often express their interest in the world around them through their play. Preparing dinner in a toy kitchen, playing with fire vehicles, and dressing as a firefighter are all examples of a healthy interest in fire. They provide children ways to explore and understand fire as a productive and useful part of life. Children this age also express their interest in fire through questions. We've probably all heard children ask how big outer space is or why the sky is blue. They have similar questions about fire as well ... how hot is fire, what makes fire burn, etc. These questions need to be addressed because children are often exposed to conflicting messages. Fires depicted on television shows and cartoons are rarely realistic! Birthday candles, easily extinguished by blowing them out, give a false sense of control over fire. That's why it is so important to educate children about fire safety and to keep matches, lighters, and other fire-producing tools away from them.

Fires and burns are the leading cause of injury and death to children!

While it is common for children to have an interest in fire, the progression from curiosity with fire to fire play or fire setting can have destructive and even deadly results. Even the term "fire play" is problematic because it implies that youth-set fires are just a normal phase in life. But fire setting is not a phase and must be addressed. Many children who set fires will do so repeatedly if there is no intervention.

Another common misconception is that if the fires set are small, they are no big deal. Often these fires go unreported. But all fires start out as small fires. And even small fires can have disastrous consequences. Any time children set fires, they are endangering themselves and others. Each year fires set by children result in hundreds of lives lost, thousands of painful burn injuries, and millions of dollars in property damage. Fires and burns are the leading causes of injury and death to children. They are twice as likely as adults to die in a fire. Many of those deaths are preschool aged children who were simply around the fire setter and were unable to escape the resulting fire.

AURORA, COLORADO -- A four-year-old little boy's curiosity with a lighter sparked an apartment fire in Aurora that sent three people to the hospital Tuesday, according to firefighters. Rescuers also had to save two family dogs.

Parents and other role models play an important role in helping children understand the dangers of fire. Children often model their behavior from those they love, so it is important that good examples are set. Children should be witnessing the use of fire only in appropriate ways such as with candles, barbeque grills, wood stoves, and fireplaces. Amusing children by playing with matches or lighters, playing with campfires, and inappropriate use of fireworks all send mixed messages to impressionable youngsters. When appropriate, children should be given opportunities to participate in *supervised* fire-related activities that help them learn how to use fire as a tool in a safe and responsible manner. Parents must educate, monitor, and restrict access to fire-producing tools.

Most adult serial arsonists and many other types of serial criminals set fires as children.

Many believe that simply telling a child not to play with matches and lighters should be all that is necessary to prevent further fire setting incidents and ensure a safe environment. But access to matches, lighters, and other ignition sources must be restricted. Sadly there are still those that believe that burning a child's hand will make them stop. But burns only create fear and scars. In order to truly help these children, the reasons behind their fire setting must be understood and addressed.

All too often these children are not given proper guidance and supervision and often repeat their fire setting behavior. Research has shown that most adult serial arsonists and many other types of serial criminals set fires as children. Sadly if children continue to participate in unsupervised fire setting behavior, the probability of tragedy increases dramatically. Parents should watch for telltale signs of an unhealthy interest in fire … matches in pockets, burned pieces of paper, burns or smoky odor on clothing, burn areas around the home and yard, scorch marks on bedding, under beds, in drawers, etc. Upon learning of a child's involvement in a fire setting situation, they should be given intervention immediately. Intervention at a young age, when fire setting behavior first begins, can make a difference and prevent future tragedy.

Children and families need to be educated about fire safety and the dangers and consequences of fire setting. Many families are unaware of the financial and legal consequences that they might face as a result of their child's fire setting. Fire Departments play a key role in this education. Youth Firesetter Intervention programs not only lessen the reoccurrence of fire setting situations but will ultimately improve the overall safety and quality of life for the children, their families, and other members in their communities.

NEWS

SAN DIEGO, CALIFORNIA -- Two teen boys will be charged with trespassing and possibly arson after setting a plastic trash can on fire at a local elementary school.

Stages of Fire Setting

The first step in solving the problem of youth fire setting is to gain a better understanding of the stages and traits of children who set fires:

Curiosity/Experimental

♦ girls and boys usually between two- and ten-years of age
♦ lack understanding of the destructive consequences of fire
♦ often have ready access to lighters and matches
♦ are frequently unsupervised

Insufficient supervision and easy access to fire setting materials often contribute to these incidents. Curiosity firesetters tend to respond well to education, redirection, and social support to not set any more fires.

Troubled/"Cry for Help"

♦ usually boys of all ages
♦ repeated fire setting experiences
♦ often have been diagnosed with Attention Deficit Disorder
♦ may have an IEP (individualized educational program)
♦ consciously or subconsciously use fire to express anger, sadness, or frustration
♦ fire setting often related to a powerless feeling related to stress or major changes in their life
♦ may not understand the consequences of fire setting
♦ will continue behavior until needs are identified and met

Often the homes of crisis firesetters lack nurturing direction or sufficient supervision because family members are preoccupied with their own conflict or stress. Successful intervention with the crisis firesetter usually involves helping the youth develop personal and social skills as well an understanding of the negative consequences of fire setting. Frequently addressing the family stressors and finding community supports are also beneficial.

BRONX, NEW YORK -- A troubled teen was charged with arson yesterday after getting into a fight with her mom and setting a fire that sent six to the hospital and left nearly 30 people homeless, officials said. The youth allegedly set ablaze a mattress after a loud argument with her mother in their fifth-floor apartment.

Criminal/Delinquent

- often teenagers with a history of truancy, antisocial behavior, substance abuse, and/or fire setting
- fires are deliberately set as acts of vandalism and malicious mischief with the intent to destroy
- schools, open fields, dumpsters, portable toilets, and abandoned buildings are typical targets

In general, the households of youth in this category may provide inadequate supervision or direction and parenting styles are frequently controlling or neglectful. Usually these youth enter treatment after being in significant conflict with schools or other authorities. Interventions with delinquent firesetters often require coordination of planning with school or legal authorities (such as diversion), as well as confrontation and restitution. At the same time, the delinquent firesetter may need counseling in personal and social skills such as anger management.

Emotionally Disturbed

- both boys and girls of all ages
- history of chronic behavioral, social, emotional, or physical difficulties
- fires may be random, ritualized, or set with an intent to destroy property
- multiple fire setting experiences

14

Emotionally disturbed firesetters suffer from characterological disorders and/or major mental illness. Their inability to manage their impulses can result in chronic conflicts and/or social withdrawal. Details of these cases vary with the youth's particular disorder and social situation. Intervention with emotionally disturbed firesetters requires addressing social as well as mental health needs. As with all children who have set repeated fires, this group requires vigilant supervision.

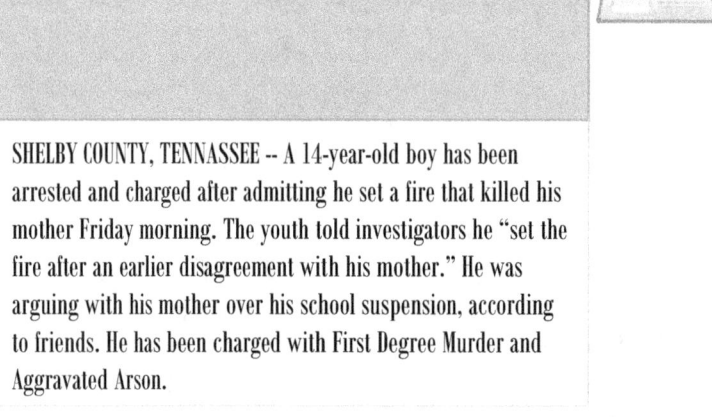

SHELBY COUNTY, TENNASSEE -- A 14-year-old boy has been arrested and charged after admitting he set a fire that killed his mother Friday morning. The youth told investigators he "set the fire after an earlier disagreement with his mother." He was arguing with his mother over his school suspension, according to friends. He has been charged with First Degree Murder and Aggravated Arson.

Studies have shown that while the majority of youth set fires are set in outside environments (dumpsters, open fields, etc.), ninety-two percent of fire-associated deaths occur in home structure fires. The majority of these home fires, involving matches or lighters, were set by children … forty-seven percent by children five years old and younger. Preschool aged children are more than eight times as likely to die in these fires. In fact sixty-five percent of all fatal victims of youth-set fires are children five-years-old and younger. According to a 2010 Consumer Product Safety Commission report, in one year, children five-years and younger, "playing with multipurpose lighters caused an estimated 800 residential fires that resulted in about 20 deaths, 50 injuries, and $15.6 million in property damage." Forty-two percent of youth-set home structure fires begin in bedrooms, often in closets or under beds. Unfortunately these "secret" places contain items, such as mattresses, bedding, and clothing, which catch fire easily.

Sixty-five percent of all fatal victims of youth set fires are children five-years-old and younger.

Statistically speaking, youth between the ages of eleven and fourteen are at the greatest risk for setting fires. Studies indicate that eighty to eighty-five percent of identified youth firesetters are male. Use of incendiary, explosive, or pressure-creating devices has increased dramatically as a result of easy access of information. Many online and social media sites provide visual examples of youth engaged in dangerous behaviors. In many cases, instructions are provided to create these devices. Easy access to instructions and information, combined with curiosity, behavioral or emotional difficulties, and peer influences can all lead to devastating consequences.

DELTONA, FLORIDA — A 12-year-old boy was airlifted to Shriner's Burn Center according to authorities. The boy is said to be in critical condition with second degree burns after one of the friends he was playing with, who was creating a blow torch using an aerosol can and a lighter, accidently fell on him, setting him completely on fire. The youth told authorities they got the idea for the blow torch after watching a "how to" video on a popular social media site.

Referrals and Initial Contact

Whether children are simply curious about fire, crying out for help, or engaging in delinquent behavior, fire setting is extremely dangerous. Children can be helped but they need the right kind of help. Understanding the reason for fire setting is often the best way to prevent it from happening again. It is not normal to play with fire nor is it a phase they will outgrow. Properly trained intervention specialists need to be contacted to evaluate each child and provide the necessary intervention. Most intervention specialists, however, are not equipped to deal with the emotionally disturbed or chronically delinquent fire setter. In these cases professional mental health experts should be contacted.

Referrals

There are two types of referrals that can be made in order for a child to attend Youth Firesetter Intervention classes. A *volunteer* referral is made by concerned parents (or adult guardians) who realize a problem exists and refer their child for assistance. *Agency* referrals include those initiated by the Fire Marshal's office, the Department of Natural Resources, fire departments, schools, the court system, and other such agencies.

Initial Parent Contact

Once a referral has been made, the intervention specialist should contact the parent and gather pertinent information such as the name and age of the child, past fire setting experiences, academic/social/medical considerations, etc. See Appendix for the *Youth Firesetter Incident Information* form.

During this initial contact, the intervention specialist can discuss the benefits of their program and schedule the first class. It is vital that the parent attend these classes along with their child therefore their attendance should be mandatory. Understanding the reasons for fire setting is often the best way to stop it but other factors also come into play. Parents need to be made aware of the consequences of fire setting, the importance of controlling access to materials that can start fires, and the need for increased supervision of the child.

THOMASVILLE, GEORGIA -- Intense flames spread quickly through an apartment complex in Thomasville, leaving dozens of families without homes. Firefighters said an eight-year-old boy was playing with a lighter while his mother slept, and caught a bed on fire.

Interviews

Before beginning the interviews, the intervention specialists should introduce themselves and explain why they are meeting. This often eases the stress levels of participants and helps develop a feeling of rapport. Even something simple as providing participants a bottle of water can go a long way to reduce the stress. We often begin our class by saying, "*We all know that we are here because of the fire setting situation that you were recently involved in but we want you to know that we aren't here to get you in trouble. We are here to teach you about fire safety and the consequences that can occur when you set fires.*" At this time the parent should be given a handout explaining the stages of fire setting and the *Participation and Release of Liability* form should be signed (see Appendix).

Interviews are a critical component of every firesetter intervention program and provide valuable information, but the way the intervention specialists conduct the interviews can have a profound impact on the quality of responses received. They must strive for objectivity and help the child and parent articulate their thoughts without leading them to answer in a particular way. Maintaining eye contact, nodding occasionally, and responding with an "uh huh" or a smile can convey that you care and are interested in what they have to

*Watch body language, facial expressions, and eye contact for what they are **not** saying.*

say. If you ask a question requiring only a "yes" or "no" answer, that's likely all you will get. Open-ended questions encourage participants to elaborate more on their answers. Asking follow-up questions to seek clarification often provides valuable information. If you create an atmosphere that is friendly, open and caring, children are more apt to open up and often share information during their interview that their parents may be unaware of ... the real reason they started the fire, other fire setting situations they have been involved in, etc. Greek philosopher Epictetus once said, "We have two ears and one mouth so that we can listen twice as much as we speak." Listen to what the youth or parent is saying. Watch body language, facial expressions, and eye contact for what they are *not* saying. Always give them time to answer and listen carefully through the entire interview.

Sometimes you just have a sense that the youth and/or parent are not being completely honest with their answers. You will find that these participants tend to talk less and their narratives lack specific details. They may not volunteer to provide the names of the people and places involved. Their answers tend to be short and often in the past tense. Their voice levels may be higher and they will often have increased eye contact. They may express sadness, fear, or happiness but their facial expressions do not match. When expressing sadness, for example, there is often a corresponding forehead expression. Of course it is always important to remember that others express themselves differently and their body language may be different but being aware of these subtleties can sometimes be enlightening.

There are a number of sources available for interview questions. The *Juvenile with Fire Screening Tool* and FEMA's *Juvenile Firesetter Intervention Handbook* both contain youth and parent interview forms (see Resources). Notes should be taken during the interview to determine the risk level and intervention needs of the child. This information will also be used later in your report. The interview process also provides opportunities for the intervention specialist to identify and intervene in any immediate life-threatening situations and report any suspected abuse or neglect. While the youth is being interviewed in a separate room, the other intervention specialist will use these same techniques to interview the parent and discuss the *Home Safety* checklist (see Appendix).

Regardless of what interview form you use, you will want to find out the following information:

History of Fire Setting Behavior
* child's age when first started setting fires
* number of fire incidents
* how the fires were ignited
* did they attempt to extinguish the fire
* did they attempt to get help
* did they hide or ignore the fire
* how did they feel after the fire (guilty, angry, afraid, sad, amused, embarrassed, etc.)

History of the Child
* have they been diagnosed with ADD/ADHD
* have they been diagnosed with significant mental health issues
* what is their school performance like
* has there been a recent stress or trauma in their life
* is there a history of substance abuse (smoking, drugs, alcohol)

Fire Setting Incident
* what was set on fire
* what was the source of ignition
* were other materials used (including accelerants)
* what was the extent of property loss
* were there injuries or loss of life
* was there a significance with what was set on fire or the fire location
* did the fire department, DNR, and/or police respond
* did the fire investigator respond and file a report
* who was present when the fire started
* where were the parents
* what did the parents do in response to the fire

"Juvenile Firesetters are the largest part of the arson problem."

National Fire Protection Association

The Family
* who lives in the home
* who was at home at the time of the fire
* who was supervising the children at the time of the fire
* have there been any recent changes or stressors for the family
* where are matches and lighters kept in the home
* how did the child gain access to these fire tools
* is the child allowed to use fire in a supervised setting
* are there working smoke detectors in the home

Based on information gained through the initial contact form and the youth and parent interviews, the youth's risk level can be determined:

Low Risk
* recent onset
* no history
* adequate supervision
* no access to matches and lighters
* no significant mental health issues
* accepts responsibility
* appropriate emotional response

Moderate Risk
* slight history of fire setting
* adequate supervision
* restricted access to matches and lighters
* possible mental health issues
* may initially have lied but admits to fire when confronted
* appropriate emotional response

High Risk
* history of fire setting
* more serious fire
* little or no supervision
* possibly family dysfunction
* easy access to matches and lighters
* use of accelerants
* recent trauma or crisis
* significant mental health issues
* poor judgment
* denies responsibility and/or seriousness of the fire
* possible substance abuse

"Sixty percent of those arrested for the crime of arson are juveniles."

FBI Crime Statistics

Very High Risk
* high number of recent fires
* long history of fire setting
* destructive fire
* little or no supervision
* family dysfunction
* easy access to matches and lighters
* significant mental health issues
* gang involvement
* substance abuse
* criminal intent
* denies responsibility and/or seriousness of the fire

Extreme Risk
* long history of fire setting
* has set many large fires
* extremely destructive fires
* no supervision
* severe family dysfunction
* has amassed a collection of ignition materials
* many different accelerants used
* serious and persistent mental illness
* altered perception of reality
* danger to self and others
* secretly proud of their fires
* has been burned several times

You will use all this information to determine whether the child's needs will best be met through your Youth Firesetter Intervention program or whether the child should be referred to a mental health agency for additional assessment and treatment.

NEWS

OLYMPIA, WASHINGTON — Local fire and Department of Natural Resource crews responded to a two acre fire Sunday. The fire began when 14- and 16-year old sisters set fire to a piece of paper. "We didn't want our mom to see the note," the girls reported. They told fire personnel that after setting the paper on fire, they dropped it the ground when it got hot. "We tried to put it out, but it just spread so quickly we couldn't stop it."

Consequences of Fire Setting Lessons

No matter the age of the child, lessons should increase participants' understanding of fire, methods to control access to matches and lighters, fire safety behavior, and the dangers and consequences of fire setting. How this information is presented and what educational materials you will use will be determined by the age of the child involved.

Preschool (2-4 years of age)

One of the most important things that is shared during lessons with preschool age children is actually to their parents … *"keep matches and lighters out of sight and reach of your child."*

For preschool age children we use the *Play Safe, Be Safe* materials as the main component of our lessons that we supplement with additional activities. This award winning fire safety program was developed by the BIC Corporation along with Fireproof Children Company and other fire safety and child development experts (see Resources). The program covers four fire safety topics:

Keep matches and lighters …
Out of sight,
Out of reach,
Out of danger!

♦ *My Friend the Firefighter*
Young children may be scared the first time they see a firefighter in full gear. It is important to explain to children what firefighters wear, why they wear it, and how firefighters help us if there is a fire.

♦ *Stop! Drop! And Roll!*
A child's first reaction may be to run if their clothes catch on fire but running only makes the fire bigger. Practicing *stop, drop, and roll* helps reinforce this life-saving fire safety behavior.

♦ *Crawl Low Under Smoke*
Children and adults need to be aware that fire makes smoke that is dangerous to breathe. The child should practice how to safely exit a smoke filled room by crawling low to the exit.

♦ *Safe for Play! Keep Away!*
This lesson emphasizes that matches and lighters are tools that only adults should use.

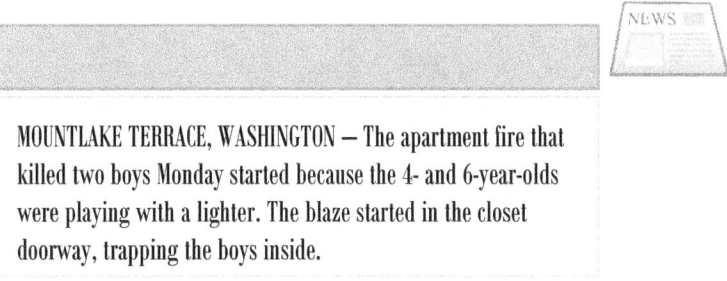

MOUNTLAKE TERRACE, WASHINGTON — The apartment fire that killed two boys Monday started because the 4- and 6-year-olds were playing with a lighter. The blaze started in the closet doorway, trapping the boys inside.

Preschool aged children have short attention spans and need a variety of activities to keep them engaged. For this reason they meet with us over four different sessions. The following are the lesson plans and materials used for our preschool sessions:

Preschool Lesson One: My Friend the Firefighter

- ◆ Read aloud and discuss the story Elmo's World: Firefighters! (Kleinberg)

- ◆ Watch part one of the *Play Safe! Be Safe!* DVD (*My Friend the Firefighter*)

- ◆ Have a firefighter put on their bunker gear and other equipment as you discuss why they need it. Stress that even though they look and sound different, they are still our friend. Practice crawling to the firefighter and safely to an exit. There are "story cards" that are part of the *Play Safe! Be Safe!* program that can be used for this discussion but a live model is more meaningful and engaging for the child.

- ◆ Learn and sing, I'm a Firefighter

> **I'm a Firefighter**
> (tune: *I'm a Little Teapot*)
>
> I'm a firefighter dressed in yellow and red,
> I wear my helmet on my head.
> I can drive a fire truck and fight fires too,
> I help to make things safe for you!

- ◆ Depending on the attention span of the child you might end this lesson by reading aloud and discussing the story, Curious George and the Firefighters (Rey)

- ◆ **Homework**: Send a fire safety color sheet* and small box of crayons home with the child. Ask parents to discuss the class and fire safety rules at home with their child.

* There are several fire safety resources that can be downloaded for free online. Our favorite is the *Sesame Street Fire Safety Color and Learn Coloring Book* (see Resources). We often copy off lesson specific color pages to use as homework.

WAPATO, WASHINGTON — Three small children, playing with matches inside a car, became trapped when it burst into flames. Two girls, 3- and 5-year-old sisters, died in the burning car. The third child escaped by rolling down a window and escaping the flames.

Preschool Lesson Two: Stop, Drop, and Roll

♦   Review Lesson One with *Play Safe! Be Safe!* "Dress the Firefighter" activity

♦   Discuss pictures of different kinds of "good" fires (i.e. fireplace, campfire, birthday candles, etc.) and "bad" fires (i.e. house fires, forest fires, etc.). We created a PowerPoint slide show using clipart and photographs that depicted "good" and "bad" fires.

♦   Watch part two of the *Play Safe! Be Safe!* DVD (*Stop! Drop! And Roll!*)

♦   Play "Safe to Play or Keep Away" game from *Play Safe! Be Safe!*

♦   Review **stop, drop, and roll** with *Play Safe! Be Safe!* Lesson Two study cards

♦   Learn and sing "Stop, Drop, and Roll" song

> ### Stop, Drop, and Roll
> (tune: *Twinkle, Twinkle Little Star*)
>
> If your clothes should catch on fire
> Here's exactly what you should do.
> STOP where you are … do not run
> DROP to the ground and ROLL around
> What do you do if your clothes catch on fire?
> STOP, DROP, and ROLL to stay safe and sound!

♦ Depending on the attention span of the child you might end the lesson by reading aloud the story, <u>Clifford the Firehouse Dog</u> (Bridwell)

♦ **Homework**: Ask the family to look around their home and make a list of things that are "safe to play" items and those that are "grown-up tools" that the child should stay away from (tools that parents should place "out of sight, out of reach").

Preschool Lesson Three: Crawl Low Under Smoke

♦ Review Lesson Two with *Play Safe! Be Safe!* "Keep Away" playing cards.

♦ Review **stop, drop, and roll** with "Fire Safety Song" and discuss the dangers of smoke.

<u>Fire Safety Song</u>
(tune: *London Bridge*)

If you get too near a fire, near a fire, near a fire
If you get too near a fire
Just STOP, DROP, and ROLL.

Do not run or jump about, don't jump about, don't jump about
That won't put the fire out
Just STOP, DROP, and ROLL

♦ Watch part three of the *Play Safe! Be Safe!* DVD (*Crawl Low Under Smoke*)

♦ Play "Crawl Low at the Beep" game (child pretends they are sleeping – roll out of bed and crawl low under smoke to the nearest exit when they hear the smoke detector beep)

♦ Demonstrate how to feel the door <u>with the back of their hand,</u> starting low on the door and slowly working up … *"If the door is hot, a bad fire is behind the door. Crawl to a window, open it and get out. If the door is not hot, open it slowly (but be ready to close it fast if there is smoke)."*

♦ Read and discuss the story, *Firefighter Gary's Safety Rules* (Stone)

♦ **Homework**: Have child go around their home with their family looking for smoke detectors. Check each one to make sure it is working properly and change batteries if necessary. Ask parents to practice *stop, drop, and roll* as well as *crawl low under smoke* with their child at home.

NEWS

LAGRANGE, GEORGIA — A 2 year old was severely burned after LaGrange police said he was playing with a cigarette lighter Thursday. The mother told officers she allowed the child to play with the lighter because she thought it was empty.

Preschool Lesson Four: Safe For Play! Keep Away!

♦ Read aloud and discuss the story, <u>Mikey Makes a Mess</u> (Kourofsky)

♦ Review safety tips with *Play Safe! Be Safe!* activity cards

Kid's tools
Are safe for play.
But matches and lighters
Just keep away!

♦ Watch and discuss part four of *Play Safe! Be Safe!* DVD (*Safe to Play! Keep Away*)

♦ Learn and sing "Never Play With Matches" song

> <u>Never Play With Matches</u>
> (tune: *Are You Sleeping*)
>
> Never, never play with matches
> If you do, if you do
> You might burn your clothes,
> Or maybe burn your house down
> And that won't do
> No, that won't do!

♦ Review with *Play Safe! Be Safe!* Lesson Four study cards, "Safe for Play! Keep Away!" or create an interactive PowerPoint game using the same idea of items that are safe for children to use or to stay away from.

MODESTO, CALIFORNIA — A 3-year-old boy playing with a lighter Saturday afternoon is to blame for a two-alarm fire that caused an estimated $70,000 in damage to the hotel he and his family were staying at.

Unfortunately you may face a situation where the family members are hesitant for their child to participate in intervention classes. They tend to believe that "fire play" is normal and underestimate the dangers involved. They may have come under protest and expecting them to attend four sessions would most likely not happen. Unless the court system has become involved, Youth Firesetter Intervention classes are not mandatory. Because of this, we developed a one day preschool intervention lesson. Obviously we prefer the four day plan, but some education is better than no education.

One Day Preschool Intervention Lesson

♦ Intervention specialists introduce themselves and the program … sign release forms … interview child and parent

♦ Watch and discuss part four of *Play Safe! Be Safe!* DVD (*Safe to Play! Keep Away*)

♦ Play "Safe to Play or Keep Away" game from *Play Safe! Be Safe!*

♦ Introduce *stop, drop, and roll* (have child practice doing it)

♦ Read and discuss the story, Mikey Makes a Mess (Kourofsky) – stress not to touch matches or lighters

♦ Use real smoke detector to practice *crawl low under smoke*

♦ Send home fire safety color sheet or *Sesame Street Fire Safety Color and Learn Coloring Book* and small package of crayons … remind parents to keep matches and lighters out of sight and out of reach.

CARIBOU, MAINE — Authorities say a 3-year-old boy set a fire that burned down his family's mobile home in Maine, killing him, his mother and his twin 2-year-old siblings.

Primary/Early Elementary (5-8 years of age)

Children in this age group begin thinking logically about concrete events and are often able to transfer ideas from a specific experience to a more general principal, although some continue to have difficulty understanding abstract or hypothetical concepts. They often have the mistaken notion that they can control the fires that they start. But little fires can become big fires in no time. We begin our lessons for children in this age group by discussing the possible consequences that could have occurred from their fire setting experience … physical, financial and legal. When going over their answers, we discuss pertinent information related to the consequences that they bring up. Parents, for example, are often shocked to learn that in our state children as young as eight-years-old can be charged with a felony.

We meet for four sessions with children this age and use *A Kid's Fire Safety Workbook* as the primary source for our lessons. Unfortunately this workbook, a product of Fire Stoppers of Washington, is no longer available as a hardcopy booklet but can be found in PDF form online (see Resources). You may copy off the pages you wish to use in your class.

We also use the story, *Francis the Firefly,* during our lessons. A great 4-minute narrated version of this story can be found on YouTube. You can find additional educational material to use with this video online as well. They sometimes spell Francis with an "e" (Frances) so be sure and search for materials using both spellings.

In addition to the above mentioned resources we also use the *Play Safe! Be Safe!* curriculum by BIC. You can find links to all of these resources in the Resources section.

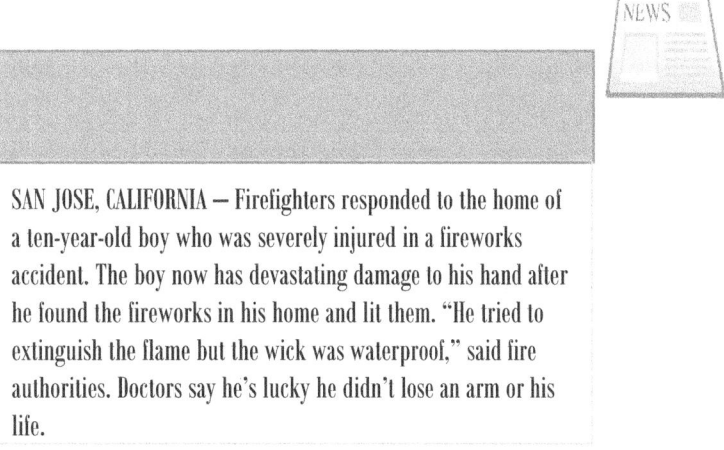

SAN JOSE, CALIFORNIA — Firefighters responded to the home of a ten-year-old boy who was severely injured in a fireworks accident. The boy now has devastating damage to his hand after he found the fireworks in his home and lit them. "He tried to extinguish the flame but the wick was waterproof," said fire authorities. Doctors say he's lucky he didn't lose an arm or his life.

Primary Lesson One: What is Fire Like?

"In less than 30 seconds, less time than most TV commercials, a small flame can get completely out of control and turn into a major fire. It only takes minutes for thick black smoke to fill a house. In less than five minutes, a house can be completely on fire."

♦ You may use the *Kid's Fire Safety Workbook* to discuss "What is Fire Like?" We chose to create a PowerPoint that uses Francis the Firefly, colorful photos and the text from the workbook to discuss "good and bad" fires, the nature of fire, and fire safety.

"Frances the Firefly is going to help us learn some facts about fire. We'll be asking you some questions when we're done about what she tells us."

 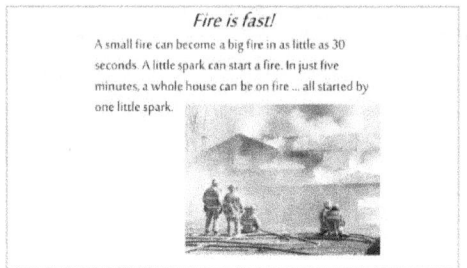

sample slides from our PowerPoint presentation

If you choose to create your own presentation, it should cover the topics used in the follow-up discussion:

- Name two "good" fires. (birthday candles, campfires, fireplaces, etc.)
- Name two "bad" fires. (house fires, forest fires, playing with fire, etc.)
- How hot does fire get? (hotter than a pizza in the oven, etc.)
- How do most people die in a fire? (from the smoke - Smoke takes the oxygen away and contains gases that can burn your lungs.)
- What is the emergency phone number? (911)
- How do you get out of a smoke filled room? (crawl low, check the door with the back of your hand, go out a window if necessary, etc.)
- How fast is real fire? (in 30 seconds a small flame can get out of control – in just five minutes your whole house can be on fire)

♦ Work together on "What Makes Fire" in *A Kid's Fire Safety Workbook*

♦ Watch the *Francis the Firefly* video (*"Francis had a bad experience once with fire. We're going to watch a story about a time when she burned her wings and find out what happened after that."*)

♦ **Homework**: Assign the "TV and Movie Journal" questions (in their workbook). Explain that, if they don't see any examples of fires, that they can think about TV shows and cartoons that they have seen in the past and use those to answer the questions.

Primary Lesson Two: Fire Tools

◆ Look over and discuss homework assignment.

◆ Watch the "Fire is Fast" section on the *Fire Is …* DVD (or online).

◆ Review "good fires" and "bad fires" and things that can start a fire (in their workbooks).

◆ Brainstorm a list of tools and their proper use (display actual tools to facilitate discussion). *"Lighters and matches are tools too and should only be used by adults."*

◆ Watch and discuss part four of *Play Safe! Be Safe!* DVD (*Safe to Play! Keep Away*).

◆ Read aloud and discuss *Fire Tools* from *A Kid's Fire Safety Workbook.*

◆ Play the *Safe for Play or Keep Away* sticker game from the *Play Safe! Be Safe!* program.

◆ **Homework**: Have the child make a list or draw pictures of "hot things" they need to "stay away" from around their house.

MIAMI BEACH, FLORIDA — A 9-year-old girl left home alone suffered severe burns Friday afternoon when she and a friend played in a shed with matches and gasoline, police said. The girl was airlifted to the hospital after the friend ran to alert neighbors. The first- and second-degree burns on the girl's chest and legs were not life-threatening.

Primary Lesson Three: Fire Tools (Part 2)

- ◆ Look over and discuss last week's homework.

- ◆ Use Lesson Four *Play Safe! Be Safe!* story cards (*Safe to Play! Keep Away!*).

- ◆ Work together on the *Fire Tools* activity in *A Kid's Fire Safety Workbook*.

- ◆ Have child complete the *Fire Tools* activities matching words and pictures.

- ◆ Read and discuss the story <u>Mikey Makes a Mess</u> (Kourofsky).

- ◆ Use the *Play Safe! Be Safe!* playing cards (*Keep Away!*) to play a Memory game (there are 30 playing cards ... the number of cards used will be determined by the age of the child you are working with ... use less cards with younger children). Shuffle cards and place face down on the table (make five rows of six cards if you are using all 30 cards). Take turns turning over two cards at a time, attempting to match pictures.

- ◆ **Homework**: Have the child draw a picture of their fire setting situation and write a sentence about what they should have done instead.

Primary Lesson Four: Do the Right Thing

- ◆ Read and discuss the story <u>Firefighter Gary's Fire Safety Rules</u> (Stone) as a review.

- ◆ Read aloud *Jerome Saves the Day* in their workbook and complete the *Do the Right Thing* activity.

- ◆ Work together to complete page 10 (*My Home Safety List*) to review doing the right thing!

LOS ANGELES, CALIFORNIA — A 10-year-old boy admitted that he accidently started one of the largest of last week's Southern California wildfires while playing with matches. Fanned by high winds and hot, dry weather, it spread quickly, driving 15,000 people from their homes, destroying 21 houses and 22 other buildings, injuring three people and blackening more than 38,000 acres.

One Day Primary Intervention Lesson

As stated in the Preschool Lessons section, sometimes families are reluctant to commit to meeting for four sessions. If at all possible try to convince them of the dangers involved in fire setting and the importance of the intervention program. But if you don't think they will agree, offering a one day session may be a workable alternative.

♦ Read and discuss the story <u>Firefighter Gary's Fire Safety Rules</u> (Stone)

♦ You may use *A Kid's Fire Safety Workbook* to discuss "What is Fire Like?" We chose to create a PowerPoint that uses Francis the Firefly, colorful photos and the text from the workbook to discuss "good and bad" fires, the nature of fire, and fire safety.

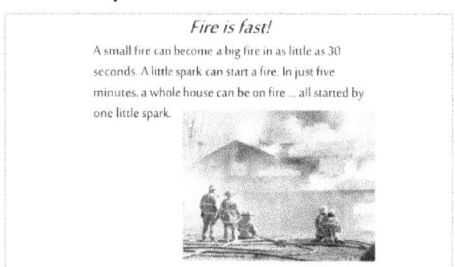

Your PowerPoint should cover the topics used in the follow-up discussion:

- Name two "good" fires (birthday candles, campfires, fireplaces, etc.).
- Name two "bad" fires (house fires, forest fires, playing with fire, etc.).
- How hot does fire get? (hotter than a pizza in the oven, etc.)
- How do most people die in a fire? (from the smoke - Smoke takes the oxygen away and contains gases that can burn your lungs.)
- What is the emergency phone number? (911)
- How do you get out of a smoke filled room? (crawl low, check the door with the back of your hand, go out a window if necessary, etc.)
- How fast is real fire? (in 30 seconds a small flame can get out of control – in just five minutes your whole house can be on fire)

    ♦ Review "good fires" and "bad fires" and things that can start a fire (in their workbooks).

    ♦ Work together on *Fire Tools* in *A Kid's Fire Safety Workbook*.

    ♦ Have child complete the *Fire Tools* activity of matching words and pictures.

    ♦ Read aloud *Jerome Saves the Day* (in their workbook) and have them complete the *Do the Right Thing* activity.

    ♦ Review fire safety behavior by reading and discussing the story, <u>Mikey Makes a Mess</u> (Kourofsky)

Intermediate (9-18 years of age)

Our experience has found that a one day session is more effective when working with youth ages 9-18 years of age. While we have worked with youth from all ages, this is the age group that we have had the most experience with. Many of those that we work with in this age group attend our youth firesetter intervention class as part of their Diversion requirements. Diversion is a program designed to give the youth an opportunity to avoid prosecution by completing various requirements. The majority of these youth have been boys, although we have worked with teenage girls as well. They come from a variety of social and economic backgrounds. They often express difficulties making and keeping friends and are having problems at school. Many of the youth we've worked with in this age group have learning problems and have been diagnosed with Attention Deficit Disorder.

Youth in this age group are going through many changes, physically and emotionally. It is not uncommon for them to be subject to moodiness and emotional outburst. Friends and acceptance by others is a big concern to them. It's not unusual to hear that they are "bored" or have "nothing to do." Their fascination with fire and how it works may now include gasoline, flammable liquids (such as hand sanitizer), and aerosol containers.

Our intermediate lesson focuses on the physical, financial, and legal consequences that can occur from fire setting. One of the most effective components of the lesson is a discussion of what the potential consequences of the youth-set fire could have been. How you respond to the answers given by the youth and family members can set the tone for the entire class. It is only natural that the youth and their family members will feel anxious about attending the intervention class.

How you respond to the answers given by the youth and family members can set the tone for the entire class.

By demonstrating that you are interested in what they have to say, they will begin to feel more at ease and communicate more easily, openly, and honestly. By maintaining eye contact, smiling, nodding your head, and simply saying "uh,huh" you are encouraging them to continue speaking. Restating their answer before adding pertinent facts shows that you are listening and understand what they are saying. Using information that you gained during interviews in your responses is very meaningful for both the youth and their parent.

We use three great DVD's in our lesson. *In a Flash: The Consequences of Youth Fire Setting* … although graphic, this true story of a burn victim is very effective. The video emphasizes that fire setting and arson are criminal and dangerous acts. Now severely disfigured and scarred, Gordon, the featured burn victim in this story, delivers a powerful message that fire setting can lead to permanent tragedy.

Unfortunately another great DVD that we use in our program, *In Their Own Words*, is apparently no longer available. I mention it because some fire departments may still have a copy. There is a free, downloadable video available from The Insurance Federation of Minnesota called *Marked by Fire* that would be a good alternative. It tells the story of a young man serving a prison sentence for the crime of arson. It shows how a firesetting incident changed his life and the impact it had on his family and the victims of the fire (see Resources).

We received the third DVD that we use, *Nothing More to Say: A Burn Victim's Story*, at a training put on by the Spokane Fire Department. This DVD may still be available if you contact them. Search *Consequences of Fire Setting* on YouTube to find additional videos that you might use (for example, OCFA's Juvenile Fire Setting PSA). *Sean's Story*, a DVD from the Minnesota State Fire Marshal would also be a powerful story to share (see Resources).

One Day Intermediate Intervention Lesson

- ◆ Intervention specialists introduce themselves and discuss the purpose of the program stressing that they are not here to get the youth in trouble but to educate them about fire safety and the consequences of fire setting.

- ◆ Explain the stages of fire setting and get paperwork signed.

- ◆ One specialist interviews the youth while the other interviews the parent.

- ◆ Provide time for all participants to write a list or short essay about consequences that could have occurred from the fire setting situation. Discuss their responses and add pertinent information. Here are some sample responses and the information we add …

I could have been hurt. (Fires are the leading cause of death and injury of children. They make up 15-20% of all fire deaths.)

Someone else could have been hurt or killed. (Sadly preschool aged children, the elderly, and family pets are particularly at risk because they aren't able to move quickly and get away from the fire. If someone dies in the fire or while responding to your fire, you can be charged with murder.)

Our house could have caught on fire. (Fire is fast and not easy to control. You not only could lose your home but be financially and legally responsible for the damage that occurs to other people's property.)

I could get in trouble with the police. (In our state an eight-year-old can be charged with a felony. Even if you didn't mean to cause damage or hurt someone you can still be charged with arson. Having a crime on your record can have lasting effects when you apply for a job, if you want to join the military, etc.)

- ◆ PowerPoint (We created a PowerPoint presentation that reiterates the consequences of fire setting)

Injury and Death

Juvenile fire setting has been identified as the fastest growing fire threat in the United States. Annual statistics show that more than 300 people are killed and nearly one-billion dollars in property is destroyed by fires set by children. Over 3-percent of the victims are the children themselves.

Injuries and Death

Children make up 15-20% of all fire deaths.

Many of those deaths are preschool age children who were simply around the fire setter.

Older children frequently play with fire outside the home, at the bus stop, or in vacant lots.

(sample slides)

"Misuse of fire can cause injury or death to the fire setter or others." (watch and discuss *In a Flash: The Consequences of Youth Fire Setting*).

Legal Consequences

Discuss arson and the legal consequences.

<table>
<tr><td>

Property Damage

Children are under the false impression that they can control the fires they set.

Nationally, children who play with fire cause nearly 80,000 structure fires per year which result in approximately 760 deaths and more than 3,500 injuries.

</td><td>

Legal Consequences

Because of the injuries and damage that can happen when people misuse fire, kids under the age of 18 **can be legally charged for being involved with fire**.

If someone is killed in a fire they can also be charged with murder.

</td></tr>
</table>

(sample slides)

Watch and discuss *In Their Own Words* (or *Marked by Fire*).

"Arson is a crime of knowingly and maliciously causing a fire or explosion. There are different degrees of arson, depending on how serious the damage is or how serious it could be. A person is guilty of reckless burning if they knowingly cause a fire or explosion."

Arson First Degree	Arson Second Degree	Reckless Burning First Degree	Reckless Burning Second Degree
Class A felony (the same as murder)	Class B felony	Class C felony	Gross Misdemeanor
Is dangerous to any human life, including firefighters	Damages any type of building, machine, vehicle, bridge, pasture, hay, fence, property, timber	Damages a building or other structure, vehicle, hay, grain, crop, property or timber	Carelessly places a building or other structure, vehicle, hay, grain, crop, property, or timber in danger of destruction or damage
Can be punished by life in jail.	10 years in jail	5 years in jail	1 year in jail
$50,000 fines	$20,000 fines	$10,000 fines	$5,000 fines
May also have to pay for additional damages if sued.	May also have to pay for additional damages if sued.	May also have to pay for additional damages if sued.	May also have to pay for additional damages if sued.

Watch and discuss *Nothing Left to Say* (or an alternative video)

"None of the kids in these videos were bad. They just made bad choices. In the first video, Gordon had been playing with fire since he was three. He said he never knew about the consequences of what could happen with one little flame. After today you won't be able to say that you didn't know what could happen. But, unlike the kids in these videos, you are being given a second chance. So it's up to you … make the right choice!"

Follow-up and Documentation

It is important that throughout the entire process, you document your work with the youth and their family. This documentation begins with the Youth Firesetter Incident Information form, includes the youth and parent interview forms, a written summary of the intervention, and if a recommendation was given for the child to receive counseling (see example of these forms in the Appendix). Your summary can also be sent to agencies that require verification of the youth's participation/attendance in the intervention course

For each youth that you work with, there should be a case record and an assigned identification number. Our case numbers consist of the year we worked with the youth and which group they were … 2016-1 means they were the first group we worked with in 2016; 2016-19 denotes they were the nineteenth group we worked with in 2016. Additional information such as email correspondence with referring agencies, fire incident reports, fire investigation reports, etc. should also be included in the case file. All follow-up materials should be included as well.

It is recommended that some sort of follow-up occur after the intervention class. Follow-up can take many forms including a telephone call, postcard, letter, survey, email, or even a return visit. We send a follow-up letter, survey, and self-addressed stamped return envelope to our families (see Appendix). Families should also be invited to any Safety Fairs that the fire department sponsors. We have found that our department Safety Fairs are a great opportunity to check in with past participants and to talk to new families. We have handouts for parents about our program and ways to keep their homes safe. Children who visit our booth are given special pencils and stickers when they answer simple fire safety questions … *What do you do if your clothes catch on fire? If your house is on fire and you made it out safely, what would you do if you remembered that your favorite toy is still in your bedroom? What should you do if you find matches or lighters?*

PHELAN, CALIFORNIA - A 5-year-old boy was being called a hero Monday for saving his grandmother's life during a fire at the family's home using lessons he learned just two days earlier on a field trip to a local fire station. The boy was one of 100 kindergarteners who toured County Fire Station 10 last Thursday, according to a news release. Along with a tour, the students were taught lessons on fire safety, including "stop, drop and roll," exit drills, and when to call 911.

Then on Saturday, he woke up coughing and realized the space heater in his bedroom was on fire, officials said. Instead of panicking, fire officials said the boy crawled down the hallway beneath the smoke and alerted his grandmother. He and his grandmother got out of the house safely before firefighters arrived.

Conclusion

It was a number of years ago when I first became aware of the problem of youth-set fires. My husband, Gary, and a fellow firefighter, Corey Dean, had started a Juvenile Firesetter Intervention program at our fire department, West Thurston Regional Fire. He would come home and tell me stories of the young children that he was working with in his program. When I began looking into youth set fires more closely I was shocked to find that the problem was so pervasive. I was alarmed by the stories that I was reading in the newspaper and watching on the evening news about young children dying in our community because of fires that either they or other youth had set. When Corey moved to Australia in 2006, I decided to join Gary as a youth firesetter interventionist. My background and experience as a teacher helped me plan and organize the lessons that I am sharing in this book. My husband jokingly tells others that he started the program but that I came in and "took it over."

During these last ten years we have worked with several children and their families, educating them about fire safety and the consequences of fire setting. Children have been as young as four-years-old all the way up to 17-year-olds. We are currently the only fire department in our area to have a youth firesetter intervention program. As a result, we have worked with a number of children that are outside of our department boundaries who were referred to us by concerned parents, schools, fire personnel, and our county Diversion program. Gary and I were given the Top Rung Award for our program, becoming the first husband and wife team to ever receive an award from our fire department. In 2014 I received the Tipton Award "in recognition for exemplary service as a volunteer and unwavering dedication."

Awards are wonderful and certainly appreciated, but my greatest satisfaction comes when I talk to children and families that we have worked with. One young man, about 17-years-old, stopped us in the parking lot of a local grocery store a few years back. He was out gathering the shopping carts as part of his job at the store but he recognized us and stopped us to talk. He asked if we remembered him and said that he had taken our class about ten years ago when he'd been caught setting fires in a nearby park. He thanked us for teaching him about the dangers of fire and how our class had really made an impression on him. "In fact," he told us, "I am hoping to start volunteering at the fire department next year so that I can make a difference in someone's life too." Another time, I had a mother stop me while I was shopping at our local mall, to thank me for working with her son and his friends in a class we had held a month earlier. She and the other boys' mothers had brought them to our class after she had discovered them using aerosol cans and lighters to create blow torches. She told me her son and his friends were still discussing what they had learned in our class. A wise man once said, "Sometimes the only chance we have to save a life is by preventing the incident from occurring in the first place." Hearing from families and youth months and even years later reaffirms that what we are doing is making a difference.

The task of organizing and implementing a Youth Firesetter Intervention program may at times seem overwhelming and as any good teacher will tell you, plans that work well with one group of children may not be as successful with another group. But, as with anything in life, the more you do something the better you will be at it. There will always be more to learn; new information continues to advance in the field of arson and youth fire setting. One thing, however, remains the same … every time a child sets a fire they put themselves and others in danger. Fire can cause serious damage, injuries, and death. One out of every three children that die in a fire started the fire themselves! You and your program could well be what makes the difference in the lives of these youth, their families, and their community.

Appendix

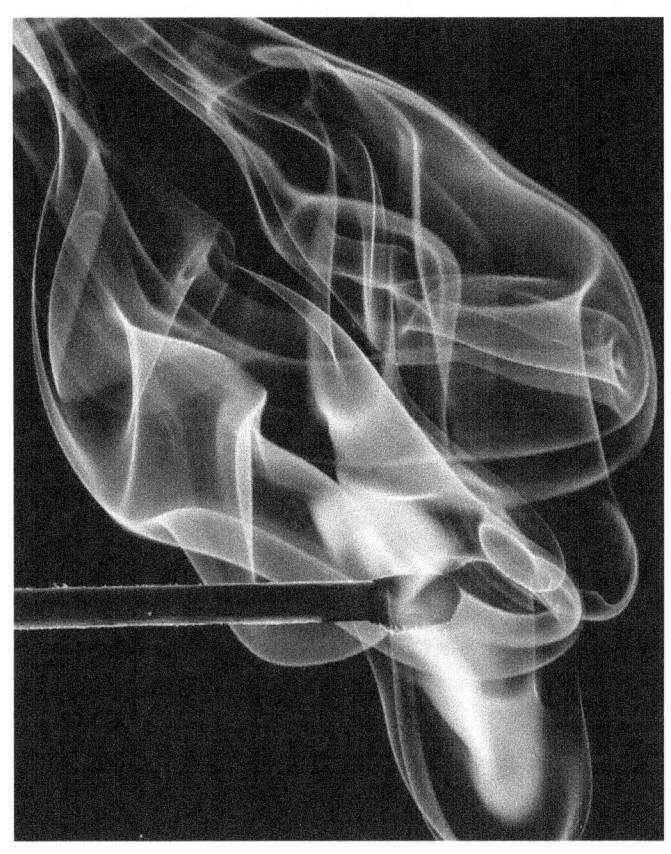

Youth and Fire

Any time a child sets a fire, they are putting themselves and others in danger!

Types of Firesetters

Curiosity/Experimental

* Boys and girls ages 2 to 10
* Lack understanding of the destructive nature of fire.
* Have ready access to lighters, matches, or other fire tools.
* Unsupervised.

Troubled/"Cry for Help"

* Mostly boys of all ages.
* Have set two or more fires.
* May use fire to express their emotions of anger, sadness, etc.
* May or may not understand the consequences of fire setting.

Delinquent/Criminal

* Often teenagers with a history of truancy, antisocial behavior, substance abuse, and/or fire setting.
* Fires are deliberately set as acts of vandalism and malicious mischief with the intent to destroy
* Schools, open fields, dumpsters, portable toilets, and abandoned buildings are typical targets.

Emotionally Disturbed

* Both boys and girls of all ages.
* History of chronic behavioral, social, emotional, or physical difficulties.
* Fires may be random, ritualized, or set with an intent to destroy property.
* Multiple fire setting experiences.

If you have or know of a child that has been playing with fire, has set fires or is unusually fascinated with fire, a Youth Firesetter Intervention program is a must to help stop this potentially fatal behavior.

Youth Firesetter Statistics

* A Youth Firesetter is generally a child under the age of 18, who accidentally or purposely starts a fire. Nearly 85 percent of the victims of youth-set fires are children themselves.

* The number of fires set by children is growing. It is a problem that needs the attention of parents, teachers, counselors and community leaders, in cooperation with fire and law enforcement officials.

* Youth under 18 years of age account for more than one-half of the arson arrests, with one-third of those children being under the age of 15.

* In a typical year, 300 people are killed and $190 million in property is destroyed in the U.S. due to fires set by children. Many times the children themselves are the victims of these fires, accounting for 85 of every 100 lives lost.

Parent Safety Tips

Eliminate access to lighters and matches

Children know where fire starting tools are located in the home.

They watch what you do very carefully and they learn by imitating your behavior.

Use fire responsibly.

Supervise children carefully

Children must be supervised adequately in order to eliminate their misuse of fire.

Parents are often surprised to learn how many fires their child has started before getting caught.

Practice Fire Safety

Teach children that fire is a tool for adults.

Inspect your home for safety hazards.

Install and maintain smoke detectors.

Warning Signs

* Burned spots on grass or carpeting.
* Scorch marks on clothing or toys.
* Finding spent matches in the trash, under beds, or in closets.
* Finding matches or lighters in pockets.
* Aerosol cans in odd places (whether burned or not).

Youth Firesetter Incident Information

Personal Information

_____   _____   _____
Date Received   Agency/Department   Person Filling Out Form

Person/Agency Requesting Service _____ Phone/Email _____

Address _____ City _____

Youth's Name _____ Male _____ Female _____ Age _____

School _____ Grade _____ IEP? _____

Has the youth been diagnosed with ADHD? _____ Are they on medication? _____

Does the youth attend counseling? _____ Where_____

Parents/Guardians

Father _____ Phone _____

Mother _____ Phone _____

Other adults in the home
Name   Relationship

_____   _____

_____   _____

_____   _____

Brothers/Sisters
Name   Age

_____   _____

_____   _____

_____   _____

(continue on back of form)

Incident Information

Did the fire department respond? _____ Date of incident _____

Where did the incident take place? _____

What was set on fire? _____

What did they use to start the fire? _____

Have there been other fires set? _____

Other notes:

Participation and Release of Liability

Based on our initial contact, it was determined that your child would benefit from our *Youth Firesetter Intervention* program. The purpose of this program is to educate children and their families about the dangers of fire and to reduce the incidents of willful and/or malicious fires set by minors. The program includes fire safety education and fire related consequences.

An additional interview screener will be used to provide further evaluation and determine the type of intervention needed. Depending on the circumstances regarding an individual case, other agencies such as the school your child attends, local law enforcement, social services departments, etc. may become involved.

The questions asked in this interview screener may be viewed prior to signing this release upon request.

I, _____, have read the previous statement and do hereby grant

permission for my child, _____, to participate in this *Youth Firesetter*

Intervention program and hereby authorize to release information regarding my child to such other

governmental entities and agencies as it may deem appropriate.

In addition, I do hereby release, indemnify, and hold harmless the _____

YFI program, all its employees and volunteers against all claims, suits, or actions of any kind and

nature whatsoever which are brought or which may be brought against the

YFI program for, or as result of any injuries from, participation in this program.

_____   _____
(Parent/Guardian)   (Date)

_____
(Youth)

Home Safety Checklist

Use this checklist to help keep your home and family safe.

- ☐ Install and maintain smoke detectors and fire extinguishers.
- ☐ Check the batteries in your smoke detectors every year ... choose your child's birthday as an easy date to remember.
- ☐ Keep matches and lighters out of children's sight and reach.
- ☐ Teach your child how and when to call 911.
- ☐ Check electrical cords for fraying, cracks, and exposed wires ... replace damaged cords.
- ☐ Do not overload your electrical outlets. Use metal case power strips that have built-in circuit breakers and surge protectors.
- ☐ Never run electrical cords underneath rugs.
- ☐ Install ground-fault circuit interrupters in outlets near sinks and outdoors.
- ☐ Unplug small appliances when not in use.
- ☐ Keep space heaters at least 3 feet away from anything that can catch fire (furniture, clothing, toys, etc.).
- ☐ Turn off space heaters and blow out candles when you leave the room or go to bed.

- ☐ Make sure you have unobstructed access to all exits.
- ☐ Store cleaning products, aerosol cans, and flammable liquids away from sources of heat.
- ☐ Have your furnace inspected by a qualified technician every year.
- ☐ Clean the lint screen on your clothes dryer frequently.
- ☐ Make sure clothes, pillows, and other items do not fall behind the clothes dryer.
- ☐ Have your wood stove and fireplace chimneys cleaned and inspected yearly.
- ☐ If you smoke, never smoke in bed.

Summary Report (Sample)

Case # 2015-009

Blaze Spitfire
123 Campfire Lane
Burnville, WA   98513
(360) 456-xxxx

Mrs. Spitfire contacted the fire department on Aug. 11, 2015 about a firesetter intervention course for her son. Her fourteen year old son, Blaze, had been ordered by the courts to take a firesetter course as part of his probation.

In our phone interview Mrs. Spitfire stated that Blaze had started a fire on the Fireside school grounds last June. Blaze was charged with a misdemeanor, placed on probation and would be required to do community service. When asked if there had been other instances of firesetting, she said "no."

We met with Blaze and his mother on August 20, 2015 for our firesetter course. During the youth interview Blaze disclosed that "fire fascinates me." He admitted to setting fire to leaves, papers, hand sanitizer, Axe body spray, a liquid car cleaner, his shirt, plastic water bottles, and a "putty like" substance, among other items (using lighters, magnifying glasses, etc.). He stated that he has been setting fires since he was eight years old.

We also discussed that his dad has been deployed off and on for many years and that the neighbor who had acted as a "father figure" for he and his brother, had recently passed away from cancer.

Lesson Summary:

The purpose of our program is to educate children and their families about the danger of fire and to reduce the incidents of willful and/or malicious fires set by minors. The main theme of our program is **consequences of fire setting**, focusing on *injury and death, property damage* and *legal consequences.* In addition, they view a variety of DVD's and PowerPoint presentations dealing with the dangers and consequences of fire setting. Participants also take part in written and oral exercises.

Based on the results of interactions with Blaze, we believe that he is in the category of ***high risk*** and is likely to be involved in future fire setting activities. When we discussed our concerns with Mrs. Spitfire she also disclosed that he is currently seeing a counselor. We advised her to bring all of this to his attention.

Captain Gary R. Stone   Kathleen L. Stone

Follow-up Survey

Child's name _____   Date of follow-up _____

Please circle the appropriate answer to each question.

How would you rate the improvement (if any) in your child's behavior since involvement with the program?	poor	fair	good	excellent	NA
Emotionally?	poor	fair	good	excellent	NA
Continued use of fire?	yes	no			
How consistent has your family been in keeping matches/lighters out of the child's environment?	poor	fair	good	excellent	NA
Have you and your child talked about consequences of fire setting since the class?	yes	no			

As a parent/guardian how satisfied were you with …

• the fire safety education provided for your child?	poor	fair	good	excellent	NA
• the interventionists' skills/rapport with your child and family?	poor	fair	good	excellent	NA
• the overall program?	poor	fair	good	excellent	NA
How would you rate the benefit of the fire safety education for your child?	poor	fair	good	excellent	NA

Any additional comments or suggestions regarding this program:

_____

_____

_____

_____

Resources

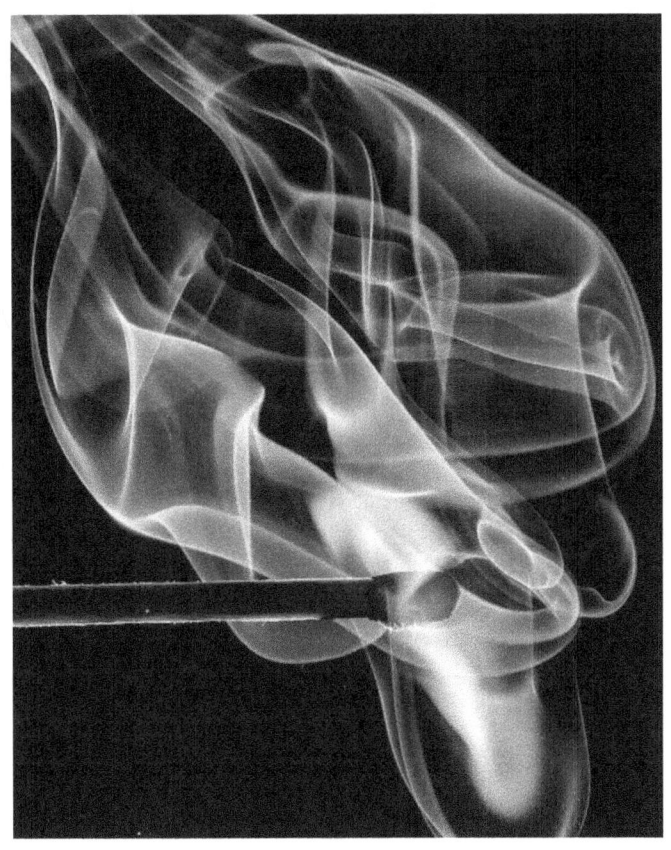

There are numerous resources available online to help supplement your Youth Firesetter Intervention program. But there are pros and cons with using internet sites. It's certainly advantageous to have "up-to-the-minute" information available but sadly sites go down and links sometimes no longer work. For that reason I have done my best to provide you with specific key words and phrases to use for searches if a link no longer is working. Here are some of our favorite online resources:

Juvenile Firesetter Intervention Handbook (Jessica Gaynor)
http://www.ccfd6.org/docs/juvenilefiresetterintervention.pdf

This handbook, prepared for the U.S. Fire Administration and the Federal Emergency Management Agency, provides information on how to develop an effective youth firesetter intervention program. Topics covered include understanding the personality profiles of juvenile firesetters and their families, identification and assessment of at-risk youth, interviews, evaluation, education, referrals, follow-up, and continuum of care through a community network. This publication also contains helpful youth and parent interview forms for interventionists to use.

Juvenile with Fire Screening Tool
http://www.ct.gov/dcs/lib/dcs/office_of_education_and_data_management_files/fa_10_juvenile_firesetters_3.pdf

Distributed by the Oregon Office of State Fire Marshal, this publication contains the youth and parent interview forms that we use in our program.

Juvenile Firesetter Child and Family Risk Surveys
http://foundation.southmetro.org/File/PFSF/6App31Ris.pdf

These surveys, funded in part by the U.S. Fire Administration and FEMA, can be used to assess the risk of future fire setting in youth. They are comprised of two sections … the Child Risk Survey and the Family Risk Survey.

Youth Intervention/Child Interview Form
http://www.firecomm.gov.mb.ca/docs/yfs_child_interview_form.pdf

The Manitoba Office of Fire Commissioner provides an alternative form that can be used when interviewing youth in your program.

Oregon Fire Bridge Juvenile with Fire Report
http://www.oregon.gov/osp/SFM/docs/Data_Services/YFPI-RptForm.pdf

This is an example of an even more in-depth fire incident report form that could be used.

Minnesota State Fire Marshal

https://dps.mn.gov/divisions/sfm/public-education/youth-firesetting/Pages/for-intervention-specialists.aspx

This site contains a wealth of information for Youth Firesetter Interventionists. Included on this site is information about *Wise Up -- The Choice is Yours* which is described as *"a great intervention tool to use with older firesetters."*

Sean's Story: My Life Torn Apart by Firesetting

http://www.seans-story.org/

The Minnesota State Fire Marshal offers this video as part of their firesetting intervention toolkit.

Marked by Fire

http://www.mediafire.com/download/qrxdnmf4z2y/Marked+by+Fire.wmv

A free download available from the Minnesota State Fire Marshal about the consequences of a youth-set fire.

Florida Juvenile Firesetting Portal

www.stopfiresetting.com

This is another great website full of useful information. Be sure and check out the "Educators" section.

The Youth Firesetting Intervention Resource Site

www.sosfires.com

You can find several informative articles on this site as well as a listing of Youth Intervention programs available in the United States, Canada, the United Kingdom, Australia, and New Zealand.

Prevent Youth Firesetting

https://www.usfa.fema.gov/downloads/pdf/arson/aaw12_media_kit.pdf

A media kit for national arson awareness week but contains useful information for interventionists as well.

Arson and Juvenile Firesetter Module: NFIRS-11

https://www.usfa.fema.gov/downloads/pdf/nfirs_q494/nfirs_module_11_arson%20_and_juvenile_firesetting.pdf

A self-study module on arson and youth firesetting.

Youth Firesetting Prevention and Intervention N0629

https://apps.usfa.fema.gov/nfacourses/catalog/details/10523

While this is a site for a six day National Fire Academy course, it includes a link to their syllabus which contains useful information.

U.S. Fire Administration

https://search.usa.gov/search?utf8=%E2%9C%93&affiliate=usfa&query=Juvenile+Firesetter&commit

Even more links for Youth Firesetter Interventionist training.

ADD and Firesetting: The Connection

http://sos.strateja-xl.com/professional-information/Articles/ADD_and_Firesetting.pdf

An interesting article that looks at the specific character traits common among children with ADD and other learning disabilities that can contribute to a child's interest in fire.

Community Health Strategies

http://www.communityhealthstrategies.com/

In addition to all of the resources on this site, you will also find the order form for the *Play Safe! Be Safe!* fire safety education program.

A Kid's Fire Safety Workbook

http://www.norfolk.gov/DocumentCenter/View/1243

This is the workbook from Fire Stoppers of Washington that we use with our 5- to 8-year-olds.

A Workbook for Kids about Fire

https://www.swfe.org/fd3-content/pdf/Children-Teen/teen_workbook.pdf

A version of *A Kid's Fire Safety Workbook* but for older children.

NJ Fire Safety

http://www.njfiresafety.com/fire-is-video-series/

Dr. Frank Field's five part fire prevention and safety video series, *Fire Is ...,* can be found on this site.

Sesame Street Fire Safety Color and Learn Coloring Book

https://www.usfa.fema.gov/prevention/outreach/ss_safety_program.html

Included on this U.S. Fire Administration site are links to the coloring book (in English and Spanish), guides for both educators and families, posters, and songs. You can even download MP3 versions of their songs! We use parts of this program with both our preschool and primary aged children.

Frances the Firefly

https://www.youtube.com/watch?v=mmflkVzAIeE

A wonderfully narrated version of the story that we share with our younger children. There is also a PDF of this story and a color sheet that can be found at **http://bucksfire.gov.uk/news/half-term-activity-young-children**.

Oregon Office of Fire Marshal

http://www.oregon.gov/OSP/SFM/pages/yfpi.aspx#Parent_/_Caregiver_Resources

Among the resources found on this page are a *Parent Responsibility Booklet* that educates parents on their legal and financial responsibilities if their child sets a fire in Oregon (but information could be changed to fit the laws in your area).

Do the Right Thing

http://www.oregon.gov/osp/SFM/docs/yfpi/do_the_right_thing.pdf

A fire awareness curriculum, published by the Oregon Office of Fire Marshal for elementary aged children.

Adolescents with Fire: Interventions for Adolescents who Misuse Fire
www.oregon.gov/osp/SFM/docs/yfpi/do_the_right_thing.pdf

Another curriculum published by the Oregon Office of Fire Marshal. This one is for older children.

Sparky's Home Safety Checklist
http://www.stopfiresetting.com/Portals/Florida/docs/SparkyChecklist.pdf

Fun baseball themed checklist for children and parents to fill out together.

About the Author

As a National Board Certified educator with over thirty years of teaching experience and a Youth Firesetter Interventionist with West Thurston Regional Fire, Kathleen Stone has seen firsthand the problem of children and fire. Nationwide, youth fire setting is a serious community problem. Fires set by children are the second leading cause of all fatal home accidents and the leading cause of home deaths among children. These statistics prompted her to become a Youth Firesetter Interventionist and to write her children's fire safety book, *Firefighter Gary's Fire Safety Rules* and her latest book, *Children, Fire, and Intervention … Creating a Program That Saves Lives and Communities.*